KT-558-473

POLAR
LANDS

CLAIRE WATTS

C152024020

**KENT
ARTS & LIBRARIES**

C15202H020

How to use this book

Cross references
Above the heading on the page, you will find a list of other pages in the book which are connected to the topic. Look at these pages to find out more about the topic.

See for yourself
See for yourself bubbles give you the chance to test out some of the ideas in this book. They explain what you will need and what you have to do to see if an idea really works.

Quiz corner
In the quiz corner, you will find a list of questions. The answers to the quiz questions are somewhere on the two pages. Can you answer all the questions about each topic?

Glossary
Words that may be difficult to understand are marked in **bold**. These words are explained in the glossary near the back of the book. If you do not understand a bold word, look in the glossary to see what it means.

Index
The index is at the back of the book. It is a list of important words and subjects mentioned in the book, with page numbers next to the words. The list is in the same order as the alphabet. If you want to find out about a subject, look up the word in the index, then turn to the page number given.

Contents

Lands of snow and ice

The polar lands are among the coldest places on Earth. Many parts are covered in snow or ice all year round. On a globe or a map of the world, the South Pole is at the bottom and the North Pole is at the top.

Why are the poles cold?
Around the middle of the Earth, the Sun's rays fall close together, making the lands here hot. At the poles, the Earth curves away from the Sun, so the rays spread over a wider area. This weakens the Sun's power, making the poles cold.

.... **North Pole**

...... **Sun**

South Pole ....

Arctic and Antarctic
The area around the North Pole is called the Arctic. Here, some animals live on the land and in the sea even during the freezing winters. The area around the South Pole is called the Antarctic. Here, most animals live in the sea, out of the fierce, cold winds. Even in summer, only a few animals live on the land because it is still too cold.

▶ Emperor penguins spend all their lives on and around the ice of the Antarctic.

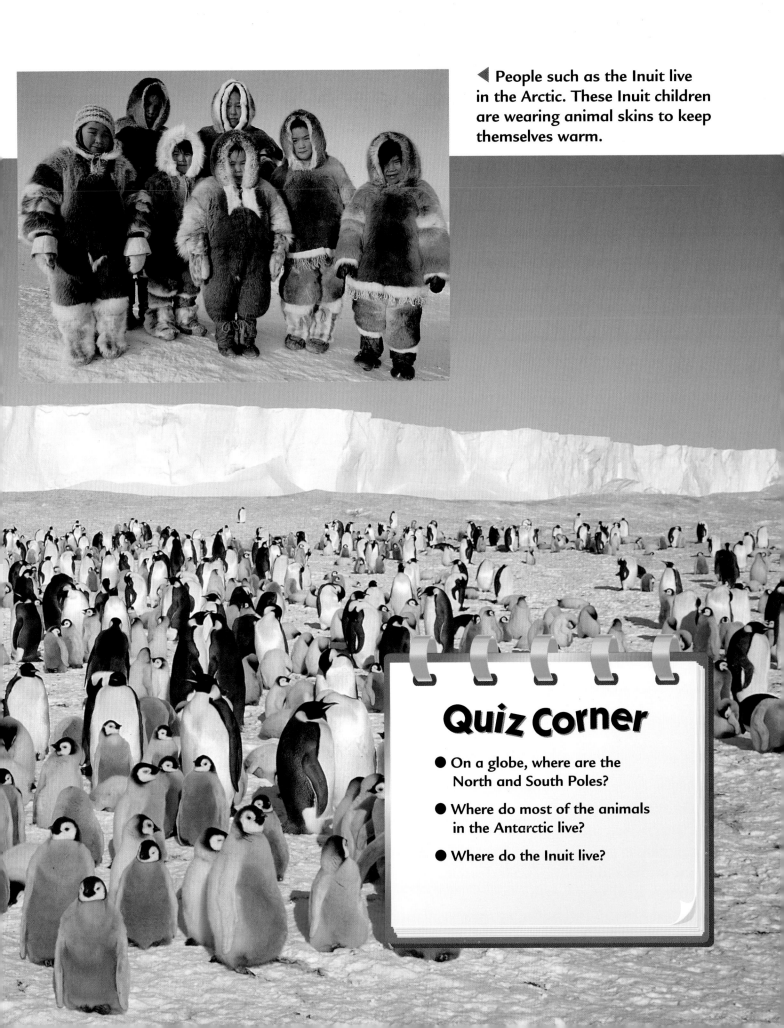

◀ People such as the Inuit live in the Arctic. These Inuit children are wearing animal skins to keep themselves warm.

Quiz Corner

● On a globe, where are the North and South Poles?

● Where do most of the animals in the Antarctic live?

● Where do the Inuit live?

look at: North Pole, page 8, South Pole, page 12

Polar ice

In the Arctic and Antarctic, there are many different kinds of ice. On the land, huge sheets of ice form. These are called **icecaps**. Rivers of ice are called **glaciers**. They start in the mountains and flow slowly across the land towards the sea. Floating ice which forms on the ocean is called **pack ice**.

▲ Seals swim beneath pack ice. Under their skin, they have a thick layer of fat, called **blubber**, which keeps them warm.

Icebergs
At the coasts, large chunks of ice break off from glaciers and icecaps. These chunks of ice float in the sea and are called icebergs. As icebergs drift into warmer water, they start to melt and break up. But even small icebergs may take more than three years to melt.

▲ Only a small part of an iceberg shows above the water. Ships have to take care not to crash into ice hidden under the water.

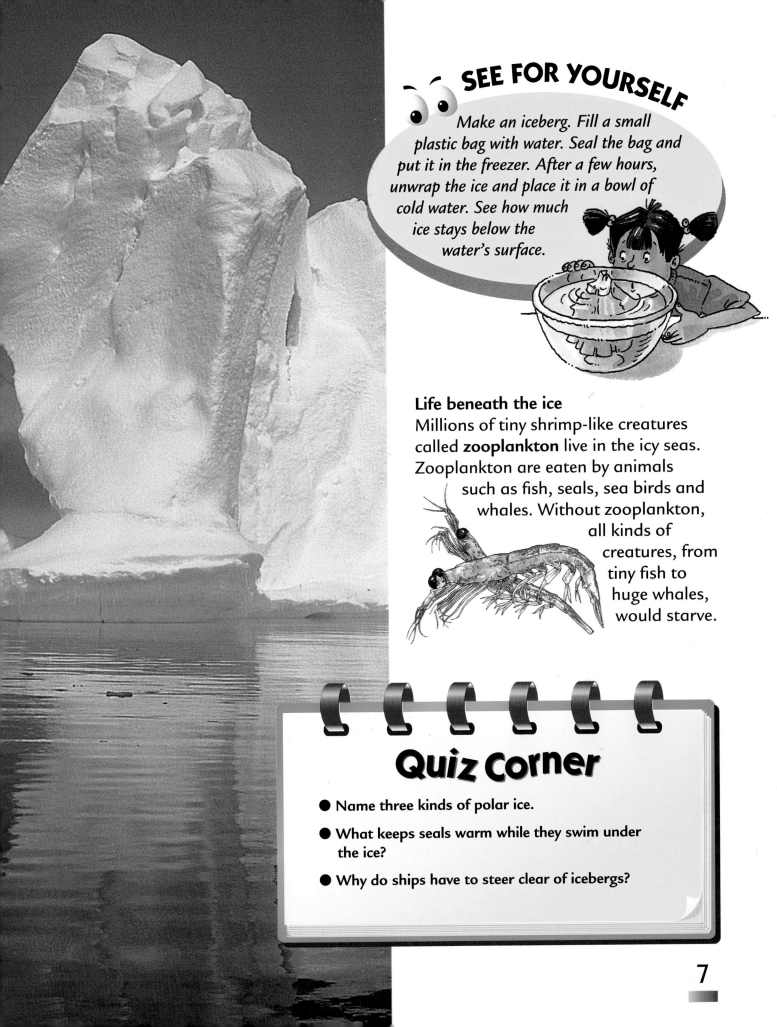

SEE FOR YOURSELF

Make an iceberg. Fill a small plastic bag with water. Seal the bag and put it in the freezer. After a few hours, unwrap the ice and place it in a bowl of cold water. See how much ice stays below the water's surface.

Life beneath the ice

Millions of tiny shrimp-like creatures called **zooplankton** live in the icy seas. Zooplankton are eaten by animals such as fish, seals, sea birds and whales. Without zooplankton, all kinds of creatures, from tiny fish to huge whales, would starve.

Quiz Corner

● Name three kinds of polar ice.

● What keeps seals warm while they swim under the ice?

● Why do ships have to steer clear of icebergs?

7

look at: Arctic tundra, page 10, Arctic people, page 24

North Pole

The North Pole is in the middle of the Arctic Ocean. In winter, a thick, white sheet of ice covers the ocean for hundreds of kilometres in every direction. Around the edge of the ocean there are flat lands where small plants, but no trees, grow. These lands are known as the **tundra**. Further south, there are huge forests.

▼ Mapmakers draw a circle round the top of the Earth, called the Arctic Circle. The area inside this circle is called the Arctic.

Ice covers the middle of the Arctic Ocean.

Much of the land around the Arctic Ocean is tundra.

North Pole

Arctic Circle

▼ In early summer, caribou start their journey from the forests near the Arctic Circle to feed on the wild plants further north.

▼ Arctic **glaciers** flow slowly down the mountainside towards the ocean.

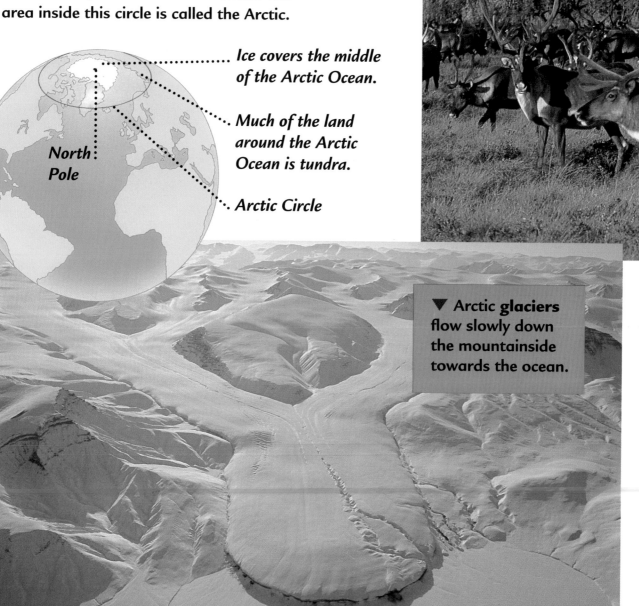

People of the Arctic

For thousands of years, people have been living in the Arctic. They live in small towns on the land around the Arctic Ocean. During the Arctic winter, people may need to melt the ice and snow to make fresh water.

CHATTERBOX

The Arctic is called the land of the midnight sun. This is because for several weeks in summer, the sun never sets. Whatever the time of day, the sun is never out of sight. For several weeks in winter, the sun never rises. It is dark all day and all night.

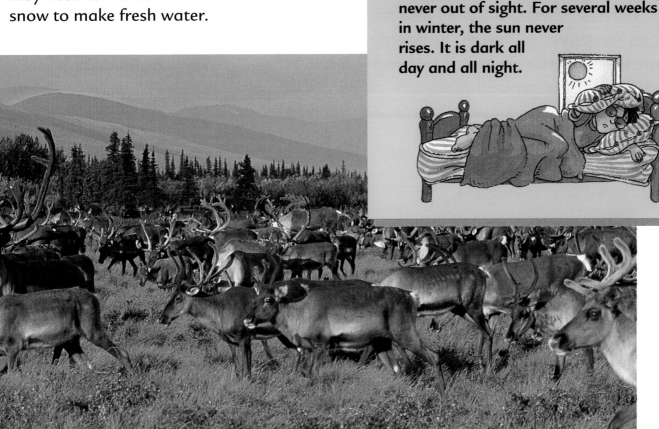

Arctic wildlife

The different **habitats** of the Arctic are home to many animals and plants. Seals, whales and otters swim in the icy waters and feed mostly on **zooplankton**. The tundra is home to small plants and many furry creatures. In the forest, wolves and bears hunt smaller animals, such as squirrels and birds.

Quiz Corner

- What are the flat lands of the Arctic called?
- Where do caribou go in the summer?
- Can you name six animals that live in the Arctic?

look at: North Pole, page 8, Creatures in the cold, page 14

Arctic tundra

In summer, snow on the Arctic **tundra** melts and the top of the soil becomes soft. Leaves and flowers grow, berries ripen and small insects, such as mosquitoes, hatch. Suddenly the air is full of the sound of buzzing insects, while the ground is a beautiful carpet of colour.

▲ The Arctic summer lasts from May to July. During this time, flowers such as this Arctic lupin brighten the tundra.

Summer pools

The melted summer snow collects in the top layer of soil. Then pools and lakes start to form. The water cannot drain away because of a layer of frozen ground called **permafrost**, which is deep under the soil.

▲ Musk oxen live on the tundra all year round. They protect themselves from hungry wolves by standing in a circle.

CHATTERBOX

The cold **temperatures** and lack of daylight make plants grow slowly. In the Arctic, it can take 100 years for a shrub to grow 50 cm high. In a warm forest, trees can grow 100 times as high in the same time!

Summer visitors
In summer, caribou and other animals come to the tundra to feed on the plants. Thousands of birds also visit. Snow geese nest by the pools and eat grasses.

Low-growing plants
Plants that flower in summer must also survive the winter. They grow close to the ground so they are not bent by the snow or wind. There are no trees here because their roots cannot grow through the permafrost.

Quiz Corner

- How do musk oxen defend themselves from their enemies?

- Where do plants grow more slowly – in the Arctic or in a warm forest?

- Why don't trees grow on the tundra?

look at: Penguins, page 18, Poles in danger, page 28

South Pole

The South Pole is in the middle of Antarctica, which is a huge **continent** almost twice the size of Australia. It is surrounded by the Southern Ocean. Small, slow-growing plants live along the rocky coastline, and thousands of sea birds **breed** here.

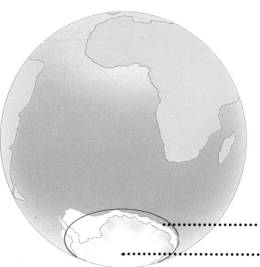

◀ Mapmakers draw a circle round the bottom of the Earth, called the Antarctic Circle. The area inside this circle is called the Antarctic.

.... *Antarctic Circle*

.... *South Pole*

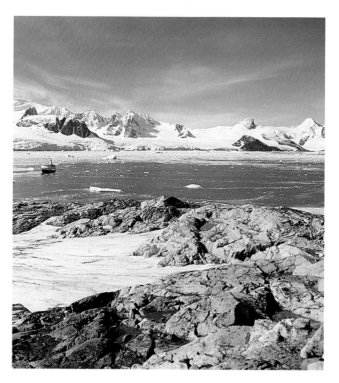

▲ Most of Antarctica, including many high mountains, is covered in thick ice. Only parts of the coastline are free from snow.

The coldest continent
In the coldest parts of the Antarctic, water freezes as soon as it is poured into a glass. As the strong wind whips over the land, it cuts the ice into spectacular shapes. A few scientists live in the Antarctic, in comfortable research stations. In summer, the scientists work outside. In winter, they work inside, sheltered from the wild storms and freezing **temperatures**.

CHATTERBOX

The largest animal on Earth, the blue whale, lives in Antarctic waters. It grows up to 30 m in length, which is as long as seven cars end to end.

Life along the coast

Few plants or animals live in Antarctica. During summer, seals and penguins come to the coast to breed and give birth to their young. Here, the babies are safe because there are few **predators**.

Antarctic waters

The temperature in the water is slightly higher than on the land. Billions of tiny plants and animals called **plankton** live in the ocean. Many larger sea creatures feed on them.

▼ Colourful creatures live in the icy waters of the Southern Ocean.

A sea urchin protects itself with long spines.

Coral is made out of the skeletons of tiny animals.

If a starfish loses one of its arms, it grows a new one.

A sea anemone catches food with its tentacles.

Sea spiders look like land spiders but can have between four and ten legs.

A sea slater has a hard shell to protect itself from other animals.

Quiz Corner

● What is the largest animal on Earth?

● Can you name two animals which come to the Antarctic coast to breed?

● How does a sea urchin protect itself?

look at: Polar birds, page 16, Penguins, page 18, Polar bears, page 22

Creatures in the cold

Some creatures stay in the polar areas even in winter. Many polar animals have thick fur, feathers or **blubber** to keep themselves warm. Foxes and hares live in the Arctic throughout the year, while penguins and albatrosses stay in the Antarctic all year round.

CHATTERBOX

People use the thick, soft feathers of the eider duck to make warm coats and bedding. But the eider duck had the idea first. The female plucks some of the feathers from her own breast to line her nest and keep her eggs warm.

▼ This scene shows the beginning of an Arctic winter. These animals stay in the Arctic all through winter.

The Arctic fox starts to grow its white winter coat so that it cannot be seen against the snow.

In summer, lemmings live above the ground. When winter arrives, they spend time under the snow, feeding on seeds in the soil.

Energy for the winter

During winter, animals have to survive for long periods with only a small amount of food. They stock up by eating as much as they can in summer – caribou eat all day and night. The extra food is stored as fat on their bodies which, during the winter, keeps them warm and gives them **energy**.

A snowy owl hunts small animals such as lemmings. ....

Quiz Corner

● Can you name five animals that live in the Arctic all through winter?

● Where do lemmings find food in winter?

● How do Arctic squirrels spend winter?

Winter naps

In winter, to save energy, polar animals do as little as possible. A polar bear spends most of the winter in its den, sleeping for many hours at a time. The Arctic squirrel also sleeps a lot, curling up in a snug burrow.

Arctic hares find areas where the snow is thin so that they can dig for food.

An Arctic stoat is called an ermine once it has grown its white winter coat.

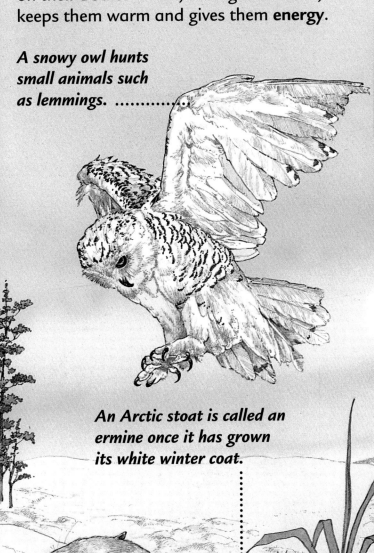

15

look at: Penguins, page 18

Polar birds

There are huge numbers of birds in the Arctic and Antarctic, but few stay all year. Most arrive in early summer, then fly to warmer countries at the start of autumn. Only a few types of birds, such as gulls and terns, are found in both the Arctic and the Antarctic.

▲ An albatross uses its long, narrow wings to help it glide and swoop over the stormy Southern Ocean.

Antarctic birds

The albatross, one of the largest sea birds, lives around the Antarctic. It flies over the sea, dropping down to the surface to catch fish. Penguins are the most well-known Antarctic birds. More than one million penguins live on the Antarctic coast.

▲ The ptarmigan has feathers on its legs and feet to keep them warm in the snow.

Arctic birds

Many birds, such as puffins and geese, come to the Arctic in the summer to **breed** and raise their young. Ptarmigans live on the Arctic **tundra** all year round. The ptarmigan's summer feathers are the colour of the rocks, while its winter feathers are white.

CHATTERBOX

Each year, Arctic terns spend the summer raising their young in the Arctic. Then they fly across the world to enjoy the Antarctic summer, which lasts from November to January. At the end of January, they fly back to the Arctic.

16

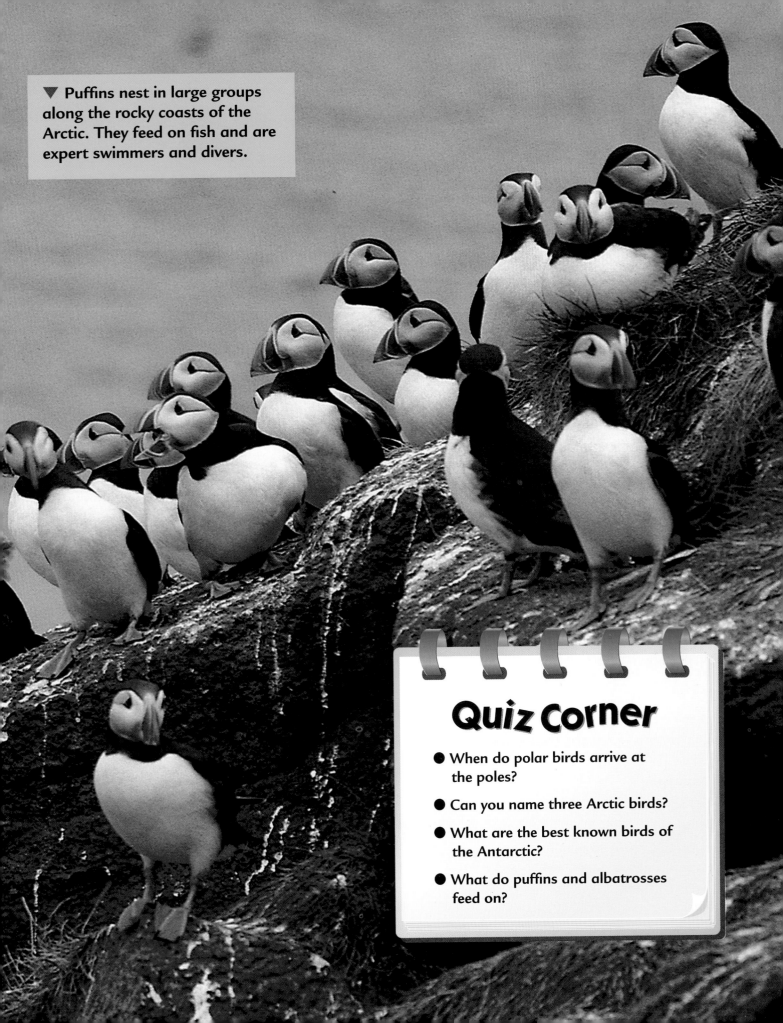

▼ Puffins nest in large groups along the rocky coasts of the Arctic. They feed on fish and are expert swimmers and divers.

Quiz Corner

● When do polar birds arrive at the poles?

● Can you name three Arctic birds?

● What are the best known birds of the Antarctic?

● What do puffins and albatrosses feed on?

Penguins

Many kinds of penguin live in the Antarctic. The biggest is the emperor penguin, which is about one metre tall. Penguins are unusual birds – they cannot fly but are excellent swimmers. They come on land only to lay their eggs and look after their chicks.

CHATTERBOX

When penguins want to travel fast on snow or ice, they flop on to their stomachs and 'toboggan', pushing themselves along with their feet and wings.

▲ Emperor penguin parents take it in turns to care for their chick.

Babysitting
In May, the female emperor penguin lays an egg. Then she goes out to sea to build up a supply of food, while the male stays with the egg, keeping it warm. In July, the mother returns with fish for the newly hatched chick.

▲ Adélie penguins feed on squid, fish and **plankton**.

▼ When Adélie penguins are on land, they stay together in large groups. When they are in the sea, they hunt separately.

New feathers
When a penguin chick first hatches, it is covered in a coat of soft grey or brown feathers, called down. After a few weeks, the chick begins to grow its shiny adult feathers.

Super swimmers
A penguin's short legs and webbed feet are perfect for swimming, and its paddle-shaped wings work well as flippers. In summer, penguins moult, which means they lose all of their feathers. They wait for a new coat of waterproof feathers to grow before they go in the water again.

Quiz Corner

● Can penguins fly?

● Does the mother or father emperor penguin look after an egg?

● What do Adélie penguins eat?

● What colour are the feathers of a newly born penguin chick?

look at: Polar ice, page 6, Polar bears, page 22

Seals and walruses

Seals live in both polar oceans, where they **breed** and feed along the coasts. The walrus comes from the same family of animals as the seal, but lives only in the Arctic. Seals and walruses are **mammals**. A female gives birth to a baby, or pup, and feeds it with her milk.

In and out of water
Seals spend a lot of time swimming. They can stay under water for up to one hour, but then they need to come to the surface to breathe. When the sea is frozen, they make breathing holes in the ice, called blowholes. Seals enjoy soaking up sunshine. They move in quick leaps on to the ice, then lie still to warm themselves.

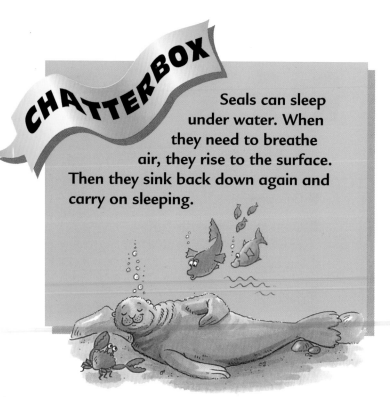

CHATTERBOX

Seals can sleep under water. When they need to breathe air, they rise to the surface. Then they sink back down again and carry on sleeping.

▲ Many seal pups can swim in the sea and move on land almost as soon as they are born.

◀ Walruses huddle together to stay warm and to protect themselves from polar bears.

Quiz Corner

● Where do walruses live?

● How do mother seals feed their babies?

● What are baby seals called?

● How do walruses keep warm?

Polar bears

The polar bear lives in the Arctic and is one of the world's biggest animals. It is twice the size of a lion! A polar bear has a layer of thick, soft fur next to its skin, then an outer coat of long hairs. When the polar bear swims, the long hairs stick together, helping to keep out the cold.

Walking on ice
A polar bear has large, padded feet. Stiff hairs between the pads help the bear to grip the ice, so that it can walk and even run across the slippery ice.

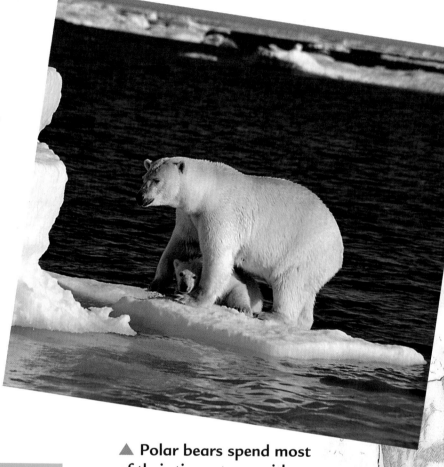

▲ Polar bears spend most of their time at sea, either floating on the ice or swimming in the water.

CHATTERBOX

In winter, when the sea is frozen over, polar bears catch seals by waiting for them to come up for air at their blowholes. One knock from a polar bear's paw is enough to kill the seal.

Hunting for food
Polar bears hunt for seals and fish in the sea. They also explore the **tundra**, eating grass and berries. In winter, when there is less food, they sometimes wander into towns. This can be dangerous for the bears because they may harm themselves on rubbish found in bins.

Polar bear cubs

In December, a female polar bear digs a den in the snow or ice. Here, she gives birth to one or two cubs, then feeds them with her milk. When the cubs are three months old, the mother bear lets them go outside for the first time. The cubs live with their mother for up to two years, while they learn how to swim and hunt.

▼ The mother polar bear stays in the den with her cubs, living off the fat stored in her body. When she finally leaves, she is thin and in need of food.

Quiz Corner

● Do polar bears live in the Arctic or the Antarctic?

● What do polar bears eat?

● Why do polar bears visit towns?

● How long does a polar bear cub stay with its mother?

look at: North Pole, page 8, Poles in danger, page 28

Arctic people

In the Arctic, people called the Inuit live along the coasts of Greenland, Canada and Alaska. The Saami live further south, in Lapland. In the past, the Inuit lived by hunting, while the Saami survived by keeping herds of reindeer for their milk, meat and fur. Today, many Inuit and Saami work in the fishing, forestry, oil and gas industries.

An Inuit igloo
The Inuit of Canada used to spend the winter in ice huts called igloos. They shaped slabs of ice into a dome, then filled the cracks with snow. Inside the igloo, the Inuit ate and slept on a platform of ice covered with furs. They lit and heated the igloo with seal-oil lamps.

window made from clear ice

air hole

entrance

platform

▲ Today, when the Inuit are on long hunting trips, they stay overnight in igloos.

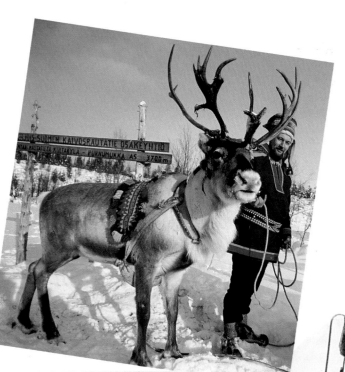

◀ The Saami often wear traditional clothing to take tourists on sleigh rides across the snow.

Staying warm

In the past, Arctic people dressed in clothes made from animal furs or wool. They lived in houses made of rock, grass or ice, or in animal-skin tents. Today, most Arctic people wear modern clothes and live in houses made from bricks and wood.

▲ Many people use snowmobiles rather than sleds to travel across the icy land.

New industries

In the past, when Arctic people needed food, they caught fish. When they needed wood, they cut down forest trees. Today, fishing and forestry have become large Arctic industries, involving thousands of Inuit and Saami. Those who work in the fishing industry, catch and pack fish to send all over the world.

Quiz Corner

● Which groups of people live in the Arctic?

● How do many people travel in the Arctic today?

● Can you name two important Arctic industries?

look at: Poles in danger, page 28

Polar exploration

Nearly 100 years ago, explorers first reached the poles. Since then, there have been many more **expeditions**. Today, scientists from all over the world work together in research stations in the Arctic and Antarctic. By studying the land and ice, they learn about our planet and how to look after it in the future.

◄ Scientists test the soil to see if it has been harmed by **pollution**.

▲ The Amundsen-Scott base is an American research station in Antarctica. Its dome shape helps to keep off the snow.

Science in action
Cold air at the poles helps to make the weather all over the world. At research stations, scientists study the wind, land and ice. They learn about the Earth's weather and try to find out if it is changing.

SEE FOR YOURSELF

See why explorers wear layers of clothing to stop heat escaping. Ask an adult to fill two plastic jars with warm water. Wrap cotton wool round one bottle and leave the other uncovered. Take the **temperature** *of the water in each bottle after ten minutes. Which bottle becomes cold more quickly?*

Preparing to explore

Just moving around in cold polar temperatures takes up a lot of **energy**, so explorers need to eat well. To keep the weight of their packs down, they take dried food, then mix it with snow or ice before cooking it. Explorers' clothing is warm, but light enough for them to move around easily.

▼ Modern equipment and a lightweight sled help a polar explorer travel alone or with a small group of huskies.

Quiz Corner

- When did explorers first reach the poles?
- What do scientists study at the Arctic and Antarctic?
- What animals do explorers sometimes use to pull their sleds?

An explorer wears goggles to cut out the glare of the sun on the snow.

Warm gloves and boots stop the explorer's fingers and toes being harmed by the cold.

Sleds, piled high with equipment, run on sturdy bases.

Huskies are useful for guarding the camp from other animals. Today, many explorers use snowmobiles rather than huskies to pull their sleds.

Poles in danger

Today, some industries in the Arctic have **polluted** the air and water and destroyed parts of the **tundra**. Pollution from other parts of the world also damages polar areas. Countries are now working together to protect the polar lands and seas.

Holes in the ozone layer
A layer of gas called **ozone** protects the Earth from some of the Sun's harmful rays. Pollution from all over the world has made holes in the ozone layer above the poles, allowing more harmful rays to reach the Earth's surface. This damages plants and animals.

hole in ozone layer ....

Sun's harmful rays .....

▲ In parts of the Arctic, people have left litter on the land. These oil drums are a danger to wildlife.

Arctic mining
In the Arctic, people have mined for coal, oil and gas that lie under the ground. They have built pipelines and roads, taking land away from animals and plants.

► Underground oil pipes damage the **permafrost** and wildlife, so these pipes in Alaska are laid above the ground.

▲ Whales have been hunted for their oils and meat for so long that they are difficult to find. They are now protected.

Keeping the poles clean

In 1989, there was a large oil spill in the Arctic and millions of animals died. In the Antarctic, to avoid a similar accident, countries have agreed not to build any oil, gas or coal mines. People would like to keep the Arctic and Antarctic among the cleanest and least polluted places on Earth.

Quiz Corner

● How have some industries harmed the Arctic?

● Name an animal that is now protected from being hunted.

● Where are the holes in the ozone layer?

Amazing facts

● Less than 150 mm of rain or snow falls on Antarctica each year. This is the same yearly rainfall as in parts of the Sahara Desert in Africa.

☆ *Emperor penguins dive deeper than any other polar birds. They can dive as deep as 400 m in search of food.*

● The Weddell seal in the Antarctic and the ringed seal in the Arctic spend entire winters under the ice. They come up to their blowholes for air, then go straight down in the water again.

☆ *The deepest layers of ice in the Antarctic are at least 200,000 years old. Many of the small plants here are more than 100 years old.*

● A team of 12 huskies can pull a sled which weighs up to half a tonne – the weight of a small car.

☆ *In summer, patches of the Southern Ocean are so full of zooplankton that the surface of the water sometimes looks red.*

● The holes in polar fishing nets are big enough to let young fish slip back into the water. This allows the fish to grow old enough to **breed**, which keeps up the number of fish in the ocean.

☆ *A polar bear has such a strong sense of smell that it can smell seals through several metres of snow.*

● Icebreakers are strong ships that break through thick sheets of **pack ice**, making a path for other ships to use. Some icebreakers can break ice more than three metres thick.

☆ *The largest recorded iceberg was bigger than the entire island of Jamaica. It was 335 km long and 97 km wide.*

Glossary

blubber The layer of fat that lies under an animal's skin. It keeps the animal warm in winter and when it swims in icy water.

breed When animals produce eggs or have their young.

continent A huge area of land. There are seven continents in the world.

energy What makes living things move and grow. Animals and plants receive energy from food or sunlight.

expedition A long journey made by explorers.

glacier A river of ice that moves slowly over land towards the sea.

habitat The place where a plant or animal grows or lives.

icecap A sheet of ice covering part of the land in the Arctic or the Antarctic.

mammals Animals that give birth to live young and feed them with the mother's milk.

ozone A layer of gas around the Earth which protects the planet from some of the Sun's harmful rays.

pack ice A layer of frozen sea ice.

permafrost The thick layer of soil under the **tundra** that stays frozen even in the summer.

plankton Tiny plants and animals that live in the ocean. Animal plankton is called **zooplankton**.

pollution Dirt or rubbish that can harm the Earth and its plants and animals.

predator An animal that hunts and eats other animals.

temperature How hot or cold something is.

tundra The flat lands which surround the Arctic Ocean. The tundra is covered in snow in the winter, but is home to many plants and animals all through the year.

zooplankton Animal **plankton**.

Index

Published by Two-Can Publishing,
43-45 Dorset Street, London W1U 7NA

© 2002 Two-Can Publishing

For information on Two-Can books and
multimedia, call (0)20 7224 2440, fax
(0)20 7224 7005, or visit our website at
http://www.two-canpublishing.com

Managing Editor: Robert Sved
Art Director: Carole Orbell
Editor: Janet De Saulles
Picture research: Laura Cartwright
Consultant: Dr Bernard Stonehouse
Artwork: Bill Donohoe, Teri Gower,
Mel Pickering and Peter Bull
Production: Adam Wilde
Additional Research: Inga Phipps

All rights reserved. No part of this
publication may be reproduced, stored
in a retrieval system or transmitted in
any form or by any means electronic,
mechanical, photocopying, recording or
otherwise, without permission of
the copyright owner.

'Two-Can' is a trademark of Two-Can
Publishing. Two-Can Publishing is a
division of Zenith Entertainment Ltd,
43-45 Dorset Street, London W1U 7NA

Hardback ISBN 1-84301-057-7
Paperback ISBN 1-84301-009-7

Dewey Decimal Classification 998

Hardback 2 4 6 8 10 9 7 5 3 1
Paperback 2 4 6 8 10 9 7 5 3 1

A catalogue record for this book is
available from the British Library.

Printed in Spain by Graficromo S.A.

Photographic Credits: Front cover: Bruce
Coleman Ltd; p4/5: Bruce Coleman Ltd;
p5(t): B&C Alexander; p6(l), p6/7(c):
Oxford Scientific Films; p8(b): Robert
Harding; p8/9(c): Planet Earth Pictures;
p10: BBC Natural History Unit; p12:
Pictor International; p16, p17: Planet
Earth Pictures; p18: Bruce Coleman Ltd;
p20/21(c): Ardea Ltd; p21(t): B&C
Alexander; p22: BBC Natural History
Unit; p24: B&C Alexander;
p25(tl): Pictor International; p25(c),
p26, p28 (l&r): B&C Alexander; p29:
Ardea Ltd.